D1443896

ALTERNATOR
BOOKS™

MYSTERIES OF
POMPEII

Laura Hamilton Waxman

Lerner Publications ◆ Minneapolis

For Nathan (lover of mysteries) and
Miriam (lover of good jokes)

Lerner Publications Company
A division of Lerner Publishing Group, Inc.
241 First Avenue North
Minneapolis, MN 55401 USA

For reading levels and more information, look up this title at
www.lernerbooks.com.

Main body text set in Aptifer Slab LT Pro Regular 11.5/18.
Typeface provided by Linotype AG.

Library of Congress Cataloging-in-Publication Data

Names: Waxman, Laura Hamilton, author.
Title: Mysteries of Pompeii / by Laura Hamilton Waxman.
Description: Minneapolis : Lerner Publications, 2017. | Series: Ancient
    mysteries | Includes bibliographical references and index.
Identifiers: LCCN 2016045765 (print) | LCCN 2016047994 (ebook) |
    ISBN 9781512440171 (lb : alk. paper) | ISBN 9781512449198 (eb pdf)
Subjects: LCSH: Pompeii (Extinct city)—Juvenile literature. |
    Vesuvius (Italy)—Eruption, 79—Juvenile literature. | Excavations
    (Archaeology)—Italy—Pompeii (Extinct city)—Juvenile literature.
Classification: LCC DG70.P7 W39 2017 (print) | LCC DG70.P7 (ebook) |
    DDC 937/.7256807—dc23

LC record available at https://lccn.loc.gov/2016045765

Manufactured in the United States of America
1-42279-26136-2/16/2017

TABLE OF CONTENTS

Introduction   A Mystery in the Making   4

Chapter 1   A Local Legend   8

Chapter 2   Going Back to the Beginning   14

Chapter 3   Secrets Revealed   18

Chapter 4   Protecting the Past   24

Science Spotlight   28
Timeline   29
Source Notes   30
Glossary   30
Further Information   31
Index   32

INTRODUCTION
A MYSTERY IN THE MAKING

Two thousand years ago, disaster struck a city in modern-day Italy called Pompeii. The city stood about 5 miles (8 kilometers) from what looked to be a peaceful mountain. Little did people know that Mount Vesuvius was actually a powerful volcano about to explode.

THE BIG BANG

It began in the summer of 79 CE with a little steam rising from Mount Vesuvius. By August 24, things really started heating up. **Molten** rock that had been building up for centuries under Vesuvius suddenly burst out with a deafening bang. The explosion released a huge cloud of hot gas, ash, and rock that rose 27 miles (43 km) into the sky. As the cloud spread over Pompeii, it blocked out the sun and rained down ash and rock. Afraid of what was to come, many people fled the city. But several thousand people stayed behind, hoping for the best.

Later that day, Pompeii was covered in a heavy layer of rock and ash. Roofs of many buildings caved in under the weight. Most people inside were crushed to death. Others scurried outside, covering their heads with pillows. Some ran for cover into the city's sturdier stone public buildings. But nothing could save people from what was about to come.

Modern scientists know that Mount Vesuvius had erupted many times before 79 CE. But people of the time were unprepared.

Mount Vesuvius wasn't the only danger in Pompeii. A big earthquake hit the area about sixteen years before the volcano erupted.

VOLCANIC SURGE

By the next day, the growing cloud above Mount Vesuvius collapsed. All of that superheated ash, rock, and gas flowed down the volcano's slopes. Gathering speed, it raced straight for Pompeii. No one could outrun this volcanic surge. No one could withstand its deadly heat. It killed everyone in its path.

When the eruption was over, the entire city was buried in about 20 feet (6.1 meters) of rock and ash. Almost overnight, Pompeii had become a mystery waiting to be uncovered.

CHAPTER 1
A LOCAL LEGEND

The place where Pompeii once stood became fertile farmland. The buried city itself became nothing more than a local legend. Most people forgot it ever existed.

FROM LEGEND TO REALITY

Hundreds of years later, in 1709, a farmer in the region was digging a new well. He hit upon something solid. It turned out to be the buried wall of an ancient outdoor theater. The theater belonged to the forgotten city of Herculaneum, a much smaller neighbor of Pompeii's.

People explored Herculaneum by digging tunnels from 1748 to 1828.

This discovery transformed Pompeii from local legend to exciting mystery. Could the stories be true? Was there really a large ancient city called Pompeii buried deep underground?

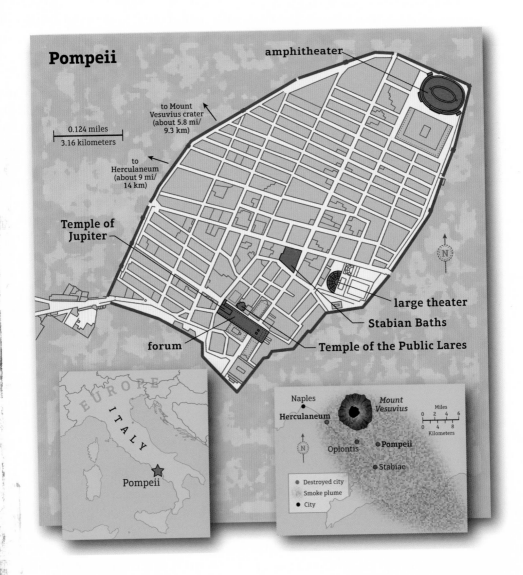

Pompeii

amphitheater

to Mount Vesuvius crater (about 5.8 mi/ 9.3 km)

0.124 miles
3.16 kilometers

to Herculaneum (about 9 mi/ 14 km)

Temple of Jupiter

N

large theater

Stabian Baths

forum

Temple of the Public Lares

EUROPE

ITALY

Pompeii

Naples

Herculaneum

Mount Vesuvius

Miles
0 2 4 6
0 4 8
Kilometers

N

Oplontis

Pompeii

Stabiae

Destroyed city
Smoke plume
City

At most ancient sites, we can find only bits of bodies or buildings. But many of Pompeii's remains were intact!

DIGGING UP SECRETS

People began to **excavate** the area in the mid-eighteenth century. In 1763 they came across an important discovery. An inscription on a buried **artifact** clearly identified the city as Pompeii. As the digging continued, people realized that Pompeii was a rare find.

Most cities from ancient times had been destroyed by weather and people. Pompeii was different. Its homes, shops, and temples had been preserved under layers of ash. Even the bones of its citizens were left exactly as they had been at the moment of death. These discoveries opened up new mysteries: What secrets did this buried city hold? What could Pompeii tell us about life in ancient times?

Ancient people used this bowl of purple powder for painting. It was found under the ashes at Pompeii.

DIG DEEP!

Most citizens at Pompeii were crushed inside collapsed buildings. Scientists once believed that the remaining victims died after breathing in hot gases. But more recently, scientists have noticed other details. They believe the curled position of the bodies, for instance, is due to the immediate stiffening of muscles that happens when a body is exposed to very high temperatures. This and other details have led many scientists to conclude that the surge of superheated gas likely baked people to death within seconds.

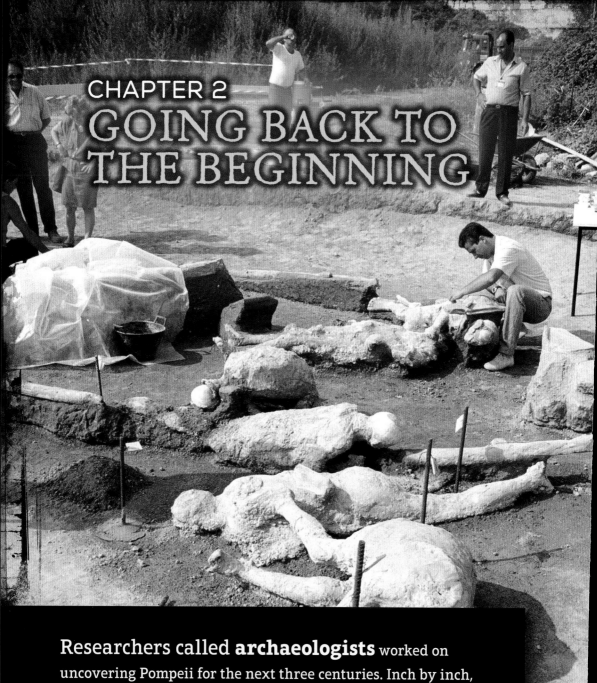

CHAPTER 2
GOING BACK TO THE BEGINNING

Researchers called archaeologists worked on uncovering Pompeii for the next three centuries. Inch by inch, they carefully excavated the city. They used tools such as shovels, trowels, picks, and brushes to dig their way back in time.

EARLY SETTLEMENT

Archaeologists believe that Pompeii began as a small coastal **settlement** thousands of years ago. It was built on land formed by one of Mount Vesuvius's prehistoric eruptions. The soil around the volcano was fertile and valuable for farming.

Several ancient empires sought to control the region. The Greeks first took control in the eighth century BCE. They were followed by another civilization, the Samnites, in the fifth century BCE. But by the next century, the region had given way to the powerful Romans.

Historians believe that more than ten thousand people likely lived in Pompeii before the volcano erupted.

A ROMAN PORT CITY

In the Roman Empire, Pompeii became an important port city. Archaeologists have found wax tablets and other artifacts that contain business records. The records show that Pompeii shipped many of the region's **exports**. They included oil, wine, wool, figs, and other goods. Another major export was *garum*, a popular fish sauce.

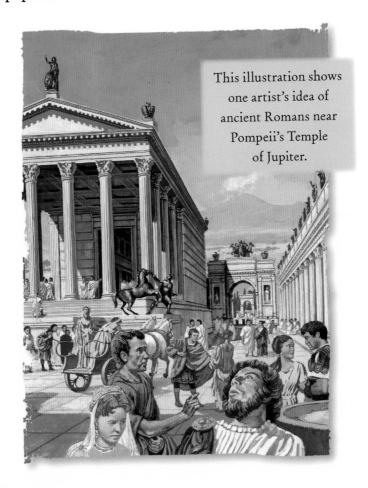

This illustration shows one artist's idea of ancient Romans near Pompeii's Temple of Jupiter.

Pompeii received **imports** too, such as exotic fruits, spices, silk, and sandalwood. Ships also brought slaves from lands that the Romans had conquered. These captured prisoners may have made up one-third of the city's population.

THE PEAK OF POMPEII

Pompeii flourished for hundreds of years. By 79 CE, it likely contained between ten and twenty thousand people. The excavation of the city showed that it had thriving shops, a wool mill, a huge outdoor theater, and an outdoor market. It also had temples, public baths, schools, and a political center called a forum. But Mount Vesuvius buried all of that in a matter of days.

DIG DEEP!

The garum made in Pompeii helped solve a mystery: When exactly did Vesuvius erupt? A Roman living at the time wrote that it happened in August 79 CE. But some archaeologists wondered if it happened later that fall. Researchers analyzed the fish remains found in the last batches of garum made in Pompeii. They discovered that the remains belonged to a type of fish available only in late summer. They confirmed that the eruption most likely occurred in August.

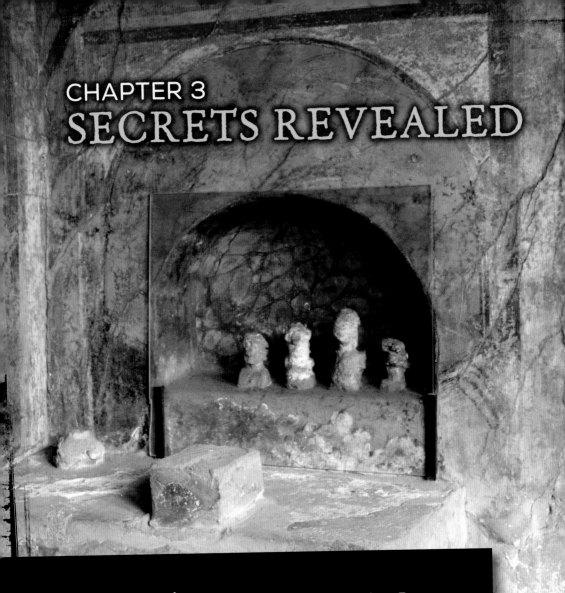

CHAPTER 3
SECRETS REVEALED

For centuries the lives of everyday ancient Romans had remained a mystery. Ancient historians and writers wrote about the rich, famous, and powerful. They rarely bothered to describe the lives of average citizens. What's more, the simple homes, kitchens, and shops of common people in the Roman Empire hadn't survived into modern times. That's why Pompeii was such an exciting find. It provided archaeologists and historians with many missing pieces of the ancient Roman puzzle.

Ancient Roman society is known for the rich meals its wealthiest citizens enjoyed. The study of **carbonized** food, garbage, and human waste in Pompeii shows that average people ate well too. Their meals included foods such as beef, pork, birds, fish, lemons, figs, lettuce, beans, and peas. Archaeologists uncovered restaurants that still had ovens, counters, and many coins left by customers. Pompeii also had at least one bakery. Dozens of carbonized loaves of bread were found inside its ovens.

This loaf of bread from a Pompeii oven had twine wrapped around its middle, perhaps so that the baker or customer could carry it more easily.

This painting, called a fresco, was found in a Pompeii building known as the Villa of the Mysteries.

WOMEN AND SLAVES

The most mysterious people from ancient times were those at the bottom of society. Few writers from the period recorded the lives of women and slaves. And few women and slaves had the ability to write.

Under Roman law, women had extremely limited rights and power. But artifacts found at Pompeii revealed that some women conducted business, owned property, and publicly supported political candidates. A few women even held positions of power in the ancient Roman religion.

Slaves in Pompeii had more difficult lives. Scientific study of their bones shows they were often underfed and mistreated. When Mount Vesuvius erupted, some were even chained so that they couldn't run away.

Archaeologists believe these bones belonged to Roman slaves who were trying to escape after the eruption.

GODS AND GRAFFITI

Romans practiced a religion involving powerful gods and goddesses. But Pompeii revealed something unexpected. Many people also honored and worshipped smaller household gods called Lares. These beings were believed to protect the home and family. Archaeologists discovered that most homes had a shrine to a family's household Lares.

MYTH ALERT!

Gladiators were trained fighters who entertained the public by fighting in large outdoor arenas. We think of them as ruthless men who were expected to fight to the death. However, artifacts and **graffiti** from Pompeii show that many gladiators actually survived the fights they lost. One common belief about gladiators does seem to be true, though. They made young women swoon. A bit of graffiti in Pompeii states that a gladiator was "the sighed-for joy of girls."

Political writing on the wall of this tavern included the names of people running for office in the year 79.

Another surprising find was that Romans created a lot of graffiti. People left these writings and drawings on walls and stairwells throughout Pompeii. Some of the messages sound awfully familiar. For instance, someone named Auge wrote, "Auge Loves Alltenus." Someone else scrawled, "Gaius Pumidius Was Here." Some people drew pictures, such as boats or peacocks. And others quoted popular poems or wrote greetings to friends.

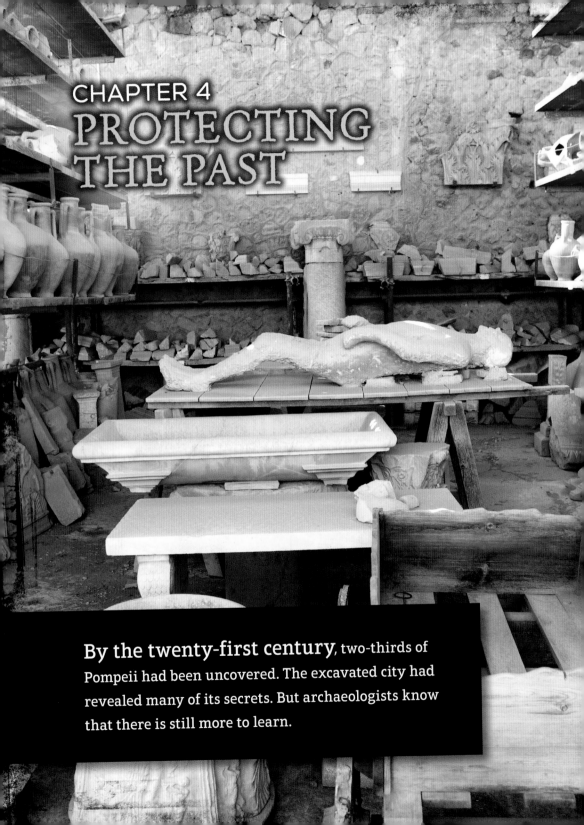

CHAPTER 4
PROTECTING THE PAST

By the twenty-first century, two-thirds of
Pompeii had been uncovered. The excavated city had
revealed many of its secrets. But archaeologists know
that there is still more to learn.

PRESERVING POMPEII

These days, archaeologists must balance their desire for new knowledge with the need to preserve the exposed city. The excavated parts of Pompeii are no longer protected underground. They have been damaged by wind, rain, pollution, and earthquakes. Tourists are another concern. More than two million people visit Pompeii every year.

The focus has moved away from digging up more of Pompeii. Instead, efforts are under way to protect what's already been exposed. And tourists are being allowed to view only select parts of the ancient city.

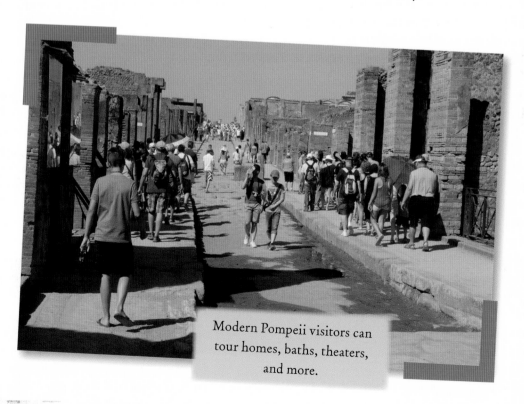

Modern Pompeii visitors can tour homes, baths, theaters, and more.

THE MODERN STUDY OF POMPEII

Another long-term goal has been to create detailed records and photographs of the city. These records will help to preserve our knowledge of Pompeii. Modern researchers are doing something remarkable with this information. They're using the latest technology to create **digital** models of Pompeii's buildings. One group is even using gaming software to re-create a 3-D version of the city's streets and buildings. That way, researchers can enter and explore the world of Pompeii on their computers.

Other researchers are closely studying those who died in Pompeii. Modern scientific knowledge allows them to determine age based on a victim's bones. Scientists know, for instance, that bones fuse together as we age. Bones also break down in predictable ways as we get older. These clues, along with signs of wear

MYTH ALERT!

People have long assumed that ancient Romans were much shorter than people in modern times. But researchers have busted that myth, at least in Pompeii. The skeletons found there show that ancient Pompeiians weren't so short. In fact, they were taller than people who live in the area today.

One way scientists try to predict Mount Vesuvius's next eruption is by studying earthquakes in the area. This data can tell them about molten rock underneath the volcano.

and tear on the surface of bones, help researchers figure out a person's age.

Human remains can also tell us about a person's diet. For example, the foods we eat leave behind traces of different chemical compounds in our teeth and bones. Scientists are analyzing samples of these body parts from Pompeii to learn more about what individuals ate.

Pompeii still has much to teach us about the ancient world. But time could someday run out. Mount Vesuvius still looms nearby, and scientists believe it is due for another major eruption. Until then, researchers will continue to work on unlocking the city's ancient secrets.

SCIENCE SPOTLIGHT
POMPEII'S CASTS

At Pompeii, the volcanic ash protected more than bones. It created a kind of hard shell around many bodies. The bodies slowly decayed, but their delicate shapes remained. They would be destroyed, though, if anyone tried to remove them or dig too much around them. What to do?

In the mid-nineteenth century, an Italian archaeologist named Giuseppe Fiorelli poured liquid plaster down into the shells around the bodies. The plaster hardened into a cast. These days, researchers are using X-rays and other imaging technologies (below) to see inside the casts. They hope to learn more about how the people of Pompeii lived and died.

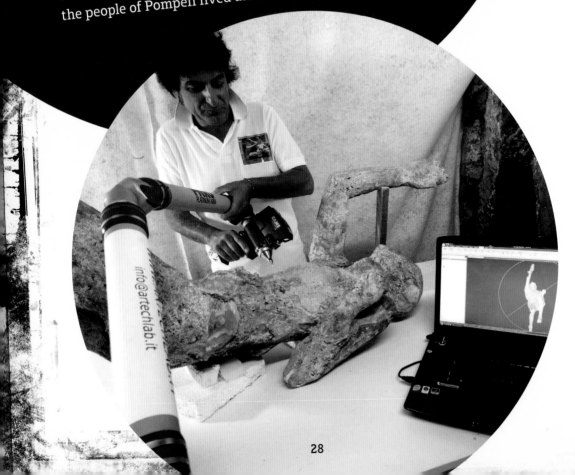

TIMELINE

800–701 BCE	Around this time, a small coastal settlement, eventually known as Pompeii, near the Gulf of Naples, is taken over by the ancient Greeks.
474	Greek control of the region begins to weaken. The Samnites start to take over.
310	The Romans begin to defeat the Samnites in a series of battles. Pompeii becomes an ally of the Romans.
Early 200s	Pompeii becomes an official Roman city.
79 CE	On August 24 to 25, Mount Vesuvius has a major eruption that buries nearby Pompeii.
1709	A farmer digging a well discovers an ancient buried wall. It belongs to a building in Herculaneum, a town that was near Pompeii.
1748	The excavation of Pompeii begins.
1763	An inscription identifies the buried city as Pompeii.
1863	Giuseppe Fiorelli invents a way to create plaster molds of the human bodies.
1960s	Major excavations at Pompeii are ended to prevent further damage to the exposed city.
2008	Pompeii continues to suffer damage from weather, pollution, tourists, and earthquakes. Italy declares that protecting and preserving Pompeii is a top priority.
2015–2016	Pompeii receives major funding to restore damaged parts of the ancient city.

SOURCE NOTES

22 Mark Cartwright, "Pompeii," *Ancient History Encyclopedia*, November 17, 2012, http://www.ancient.eu/pompeii/.

23 Doug Stewart, "Resurrecting Pompeii," *Smithsonian*, February 2006, http://www.smithsonianmag.com/history/resurrecting-pompeii -109163501/?no-ist=&onsite_campaign=photogalleries&page=3.

GLOSSARY

archaeologists: people who study human history by digging up and studying ancient buildings, objects, and human remains

artifact: a historical object made by humans

carbonized: turned into a hard, natural material called carbon due to exposure to extremely high temperatures. Bread, food, and other items were carbonized during Pompeii's volcanic surge.

digital: created by and used with computer technology

excavate: to dig in the earth in search of buried remains

exports: goods sold to other regions, countries, or civilizations

graffiti: writings and other markings scratched or written on the walls of buildings and other public places

imports: goods purchased from other regions, countries, or civilizations

molten: liquid. Underground rock becomes molten due to the high temperature and pressure beneath Earth's surface.

settlement: a place where people have built a new community

FURTHER INFORMATION

Doeden, Matt. *Tools and Treasures of Ancient Rome*. Minneapolis: Lerner Publications, 2014.

Huey, Lois Minor. *Children of the Past: Archaeology and the Lives of Kids*. Minneapolis: Millbrook Press, 2017.

Levy, Janey. *The City of Pompeii*. New York: Gareth Stevens, 2016.

Plaster Citizens of Pompeii
http://www.atlasobscura.com/places/plaster-citizens-of-pompeii

Pompeii
http://www.history.com/topics/ancient-history/pompeii

Pompeii Photos: Archaeologists Find Skeletal Remains of Victims of Vesuvius Eruption
http://www.livescience.com/55205-photos-more-victims-pompeii
-vesuvius-eruption.html

Pompeii: Portents of Disaster
http://www.bbc.co.uk/history/ancient/romans/pompeii_portents_01
.shtml

Woolf, Alex. *Meet the Ancient Romans*. New York: Gareth Stevens, 2015.

INDEX

buildings, 6, 9, 12, 13, 17, 19, 26

causes of death, 6–7, 13

digital research, 26

excavation, 11–12, 14, 17, 24–25

food, 16, 17, 19, 27

gladiators, 22

graffiti, 22, 23

Herculaneum, 9

Mount Vesuvius, 4–7, 27

religion, 21, 22

Roman Empire, 15–16, 19

Romans, 15–23, 26–27

slaves, 16, 20–21

tourists, 25

women's lives, 20–21

PHOTO ACKNOWLEDGMENTS

The images in this book are used with the permission of: © Gordan/ Shutterstock.com (grunge border texture) © Girolamo Cracchiolo/Moment Open/ Getty Images, p. 1; © Demetrio Carrasco/AWL Images RM/Getty Images, pp. 4–5; © Louis Jean Desprez/Getty Images, p. 6; © Alex Gore/Alamy, p. 7; © Wellcome Library, London/Wikimedia Commons (CC BY 4.0), p. 8; © Chronicle/Alamy, p. 9; © Laura Westlund/Independent Picture Service, p. 10; © Keith Heron/Alamy, p. 11; © L. Pedicini/DeAgostini/Getty Images, p. 12; © Julian Money-Kyrle/Alamy, p. 13; AP Photo, p. 14; © Look and Learn/Bridgeman Images, pp. 15, 16; © robertharding/ Alamy, pp. 18, 27; © De Agostini Picture Library/Getty Images, p. 19; © SuperStock/ Alamy, p. 20; © Werner Forman/Universal Images Group/Getty Images, p. 21; © Tony Lilley/Alamy, p. 23; © Mirko Angeli/Alamy, p. 24; © Jack Barker/Alamy, p. 25; © AGENZIA SINTESI/Alamy, p. 28.

Front cover: © Girolamo Cracchiolo/Moment Open/Getty Images; © Gordan/ Shutterstock.com (grunge border texture).